Creative (☆) Editions

Text copyright © 2021 by J. Patrick Lewis · Illustrations copyright © 2021 by Miriam Nerlove
Edited by Kate Riggs · Designed by Rita Marshall · Published in 2021 by Creative Editions
P.O. Box 227, Mankato, MN 56002 USA · Creative Editions is an imprint of The Creative Company
www.thecreativecompany.us · All rights reserved. No part of the contents of this book may be
reproduced by any means without the written permission of the publisher. Printed in China
Library of Congress Cataloging-in-Publication Data
Names: Lewis, J. Patrick, author. / Nerlove, Miriam, illustrator.
Title: I am elephant / by J. Patrick Lewis; illustrated by Miriam Nerlove.
Summary: Elephants, with their matriarchal societies, long memories, and demonstrations
of emotional connections, are some of the world's most treasured animals. However, they
are also among the most threatened. It is up to humans to protect them before it is too late.
Identifiers: LCCN 2020053412 / ISBN 978-1-56846-378-0
Subjects: LCSH: Elephants—Juvenile literature.
Classification: LCC QL737.P98 L495 2021   DDC 599.67—dc23
First edition 9 8 7 6 5 4 3 2 1

J. Patrick Lewis illustrated by Miriam Nerlove

I AM ELEPHANT

I am Elephant.

Queen of the Grasslands,

Matriarch of
Tropical Forests,

Delight of the
imagination.

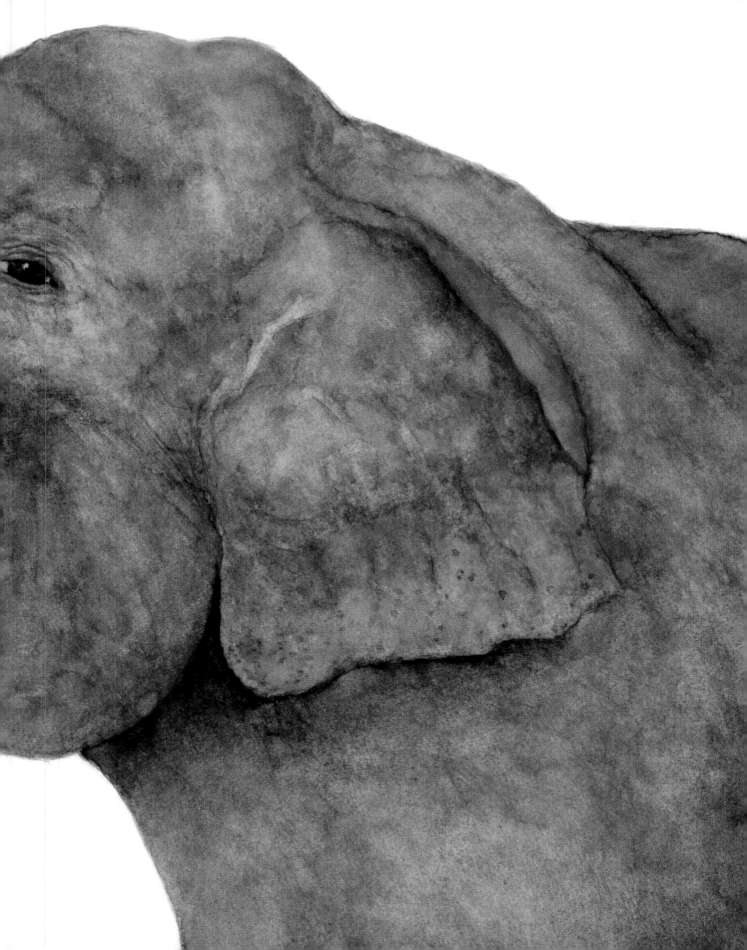

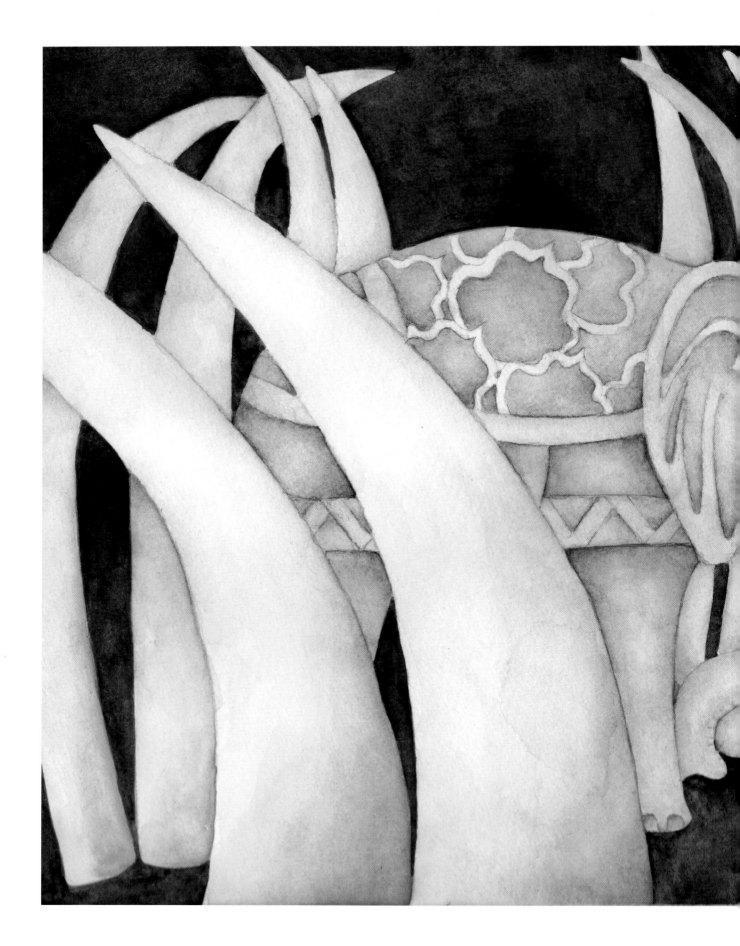

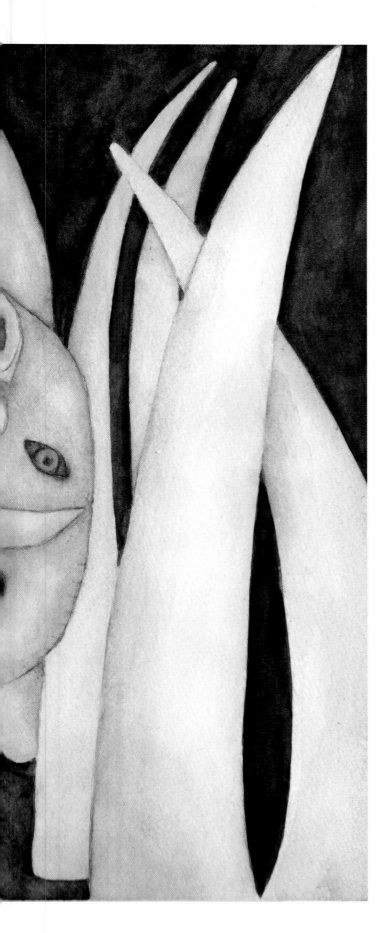

The word *elephant* comes from the Greek *elephas*, meaning *ivory*.

At my birth I was the jewel
of my mother's eye,
fussed over by all females
and juveniles of my family—
the family I will never leave.

Someday, I will be
like my mother and
grandmother—
slow-motion majesty.

AFRICA

My ears resemble the continent of Africa; they are larger than my Asian cousins' ears, shaped like the outline of India.

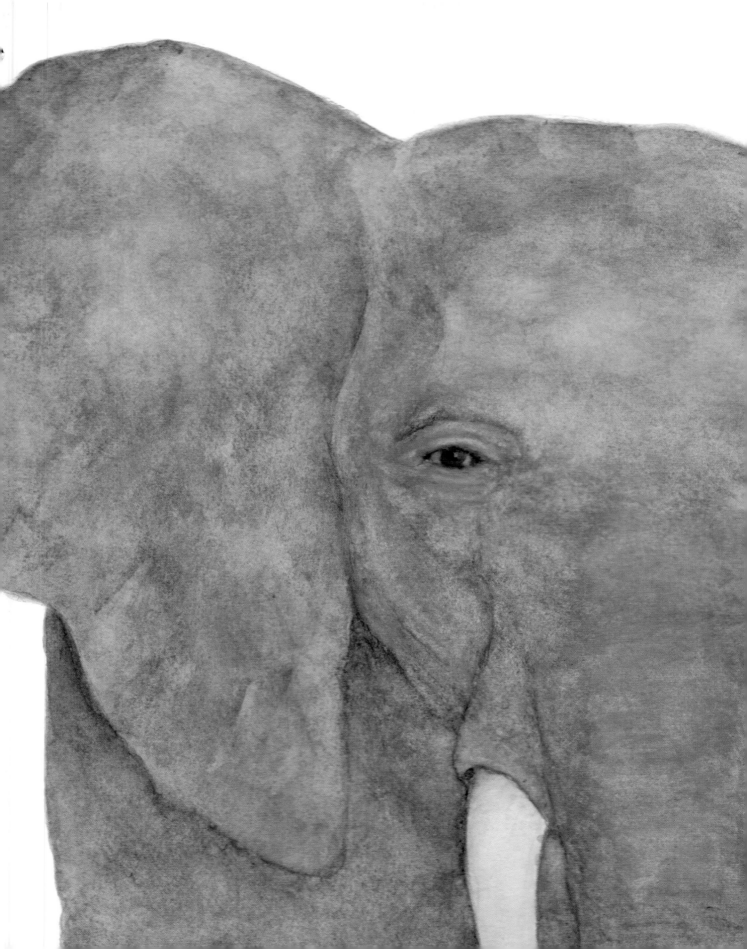

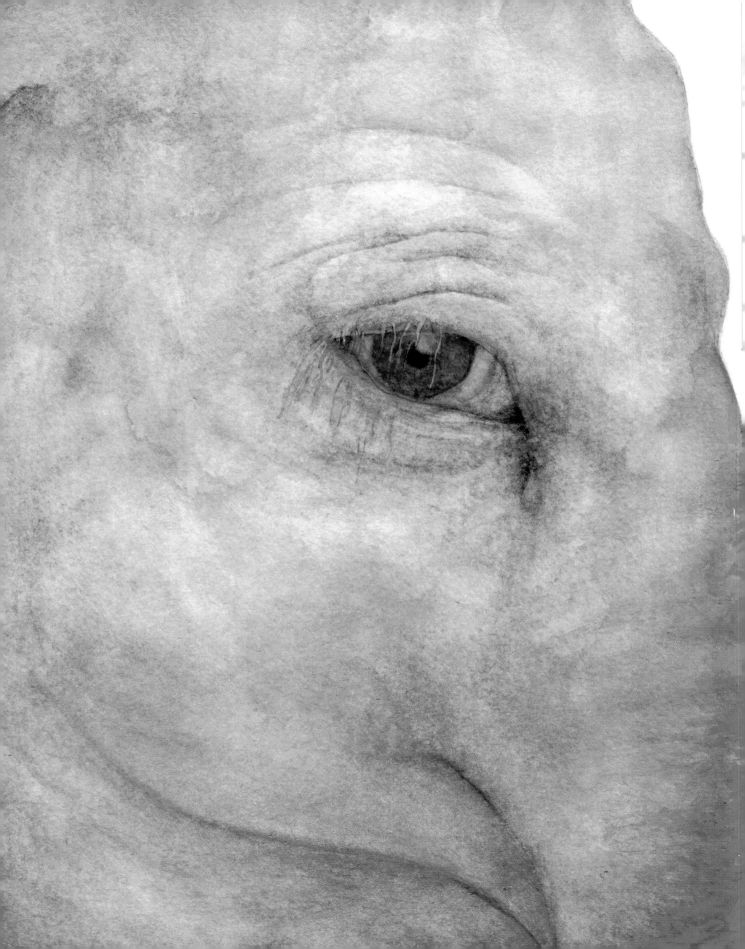

I show love and
caring by touch;
sadness and grief
through tears.

For Hindus,

I am wealth and prosperity.

(How true.)

For Buddhists,

I am patience,

strength, loyalty,

and wisdom.

To children, I am the spectacle of wonder and awe, looming large in their dreams.

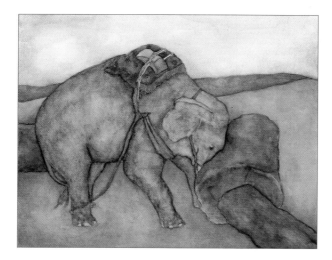

To the cruel and the ignorant,

I am a beast of burden,

a circus sideshow,

a freak of nature . . . ,

nothing more.

At 60 or so, I will die
a natural death,
too weak to chew
any longer.

If I am lucky, I will die
near the place of my
birth . . .

free from human
chains.

Elephants are the largest land animals on Earth, found in 37 countries in sub-Saharan Africa, as well as in India and throughout much of Southeast Asia. Today, there are approximately 400,000 African and 40,000 Asian elephants in existence. They live to be about 60 to 70 years old in the wild. The African forest elephant and African bush (or savanna) elephant are considered "vulnerable," and their Asian cousin is classified as "endangered," according to the International Union for Conservation of Nature (IUCN). Poachers kill approximately 100 African elephants for their tusks every day.

A male African bush elephant can be 13 feet (4 m) tall. Asian elephants reach heights of 6.6 to 9.8 feet (2–3 m). All elephants display a remarkable sense of smell but have poor eyesight. These huge beasts are herbivores, eating plants, leaves, bark, shrubs, and tree fruits. They are integral parts of their ecosystems.